THE REALITIES THAT EVERY BELIEVER AND NON-BELIEVER WILL DEAL WITH AFTER MARRIAGE

Table of Content

Introduction

DEDICATION

This book is dedicated to the late Willie Smith Jr and Betty Ann Smith, my beloved parents who through their example showed me what a marriage is suppose to look like and who took the time to instill in me principles that are important in being a good husband and a Christ-centered man.

To Mr. Floyd Rorie and Mrs. Johnnie Mae Rorie who are my father-in-law and mother-in-law to be. Thank you for taking the time to discuss what it takes to have a successful marriage and for showing me how 50 years of marriage can be fulfilled with love in the midst of all and any circumstances as long as you respect each other. Thank you also for accepting me into your family and giving me the hand of your beautiful daughter Tonya in marriage (forth coming).

Introduction

In case you have not heard the news yet, the divorce rate in America is out of control. Worst, in my opinion is the fact that the divorce rate among Christians is just as high or worst.

For the record, I am no exception when it comes to Christians who have gone through divorce and I certainly don't excuse myself when I talk about how bad this issue is, but I think that the fact that I have experienced it myself makes me a good candidate to

discuss the issues from a realistic perspective.

This is not a book about me and it is not an opportunity for me to blow my horn and bash anyone that may have been involved in my past dilemma(s). This book is designed to help married people have a platform to understand some of the things that may help save that marriages as I too could have used them during my challenging moments. Fortunately for me they are things that I have learned and that I am adopting for my marriage.

Marriage can be beautiful. Marriage can be eternal. Marriage can be the driving force in your life if you really want it to be.

My soon to be father-in-law and mother –in-law have been together for 50 years. One day, I asked them what the secret to a long marriage was and they both replied, "We respect each other."

I was privileged to have watched my father and mother live together in marriage until my father died in 1988. By that time they had been married for 28 years. I cannot ever remember a time when my parents fought, nor can I boast that it was a marriage that did not have a few bumps in the road, but they did exemplify a couple who were committed to being together forever.

As you read this book it is my prayer that you read it as a couple and discuss the content of it in an effort to improve your marriage if it is in need of such. I encourage you to prayer about the content and ask God how you can use this not only for yourself but for others who may be in need of understanding. Perhaps God will use you to discuss these topics among your friends who

are married in a setting that may help heal marriages. Whatever the case may be, know that God wants the marriages of His children to work.

CHAPTER 1

WHAT IS MARRIAGE?

If you really want to know what a marriage is you can start in Genesis 2:21. This passage(s) depicts a time when God had furnished man with what was necessary for him to carry out a purpose, but God realized that Adams profession could never take the place of the void that would be within him unless he, Adam had someone of his "kind" to walk along side of him.

God in his great wisdom took a part of man and made for man a "help meet." That is, one that is capable of helping Adam to be all he could be as God had ordained. He presented this gift to Adam and gladly accepted this gift because he knew it would compliment and not complicate his life.

Thus we have what many believe to be the first marriage.

I want you to notice three things about this marriage:

1. It was divine before it was natural. That is, it was in the mind of God before he made it manifest outwardly.

2. God himself sanctioned this union and he placed at least one common thing that was mutual to them both.

3. God presented it to him and it was a monogamous relationship.

That is what made it a perfect union, it had those three components. I did not say it was perfect in the sense that there were no issues. The fact that they transgressed makes it clear that there was at least one issue. On the other hand, that issue was not enough to make them lose what God had ordained.

What exactly is marriage? Marriage, according to Merriam Webster is the state of being united to a person of the opposite sex as husband and wife in a consensual and contractual relationship recognized by law.

I was fortunate to get another definition that I like that was written by Daniel Freeman in his book, Why Get Married?

Mr. Freeman states, " Marriage is a relationship between man and woman intended by God to be a monogamous relationship, intended to be a permanent bond in which many needs are satisfied-the need to love and be loved, the need for deep friendship, for sharing, for companionship, for sexual satisfaction, for children, the need to escape loneliness. Marriage ought to be a bond of love, reflecting the love Christ has for His people, a bond of sacrificial love where husband and wife have become one, one flesh, a unity."

I wholeheartedly agree with Mr. Freeman and even though I cannot boast that I am not a victim of the "D" word, I have had time to pray and meditate on what I could have done and what it was that I did not know or consider then that I do now.

In the book of Malachi, chapter 2:14 marriage is called a covenant.

What is a covenant? A covenant is a legally binding relationship. Unlike a contract, when you enter covenant you enter it with the intent to have an intimate relationship present. That means that whatever happens in the marriage must be based on the relationship that you have with the other person.

Do you remember the marriage vows? If you used the standard one then you made covenant to live together in holy covenant marriage, to love each other, to comfort each other, to honor and keep each other, in sickness and in health and forsaking all others and to be faith to each other until death do you part. Remember those? That was covenant. That was what you committed to do to each other for the rest of your life. There were two people making covenant at that altar and that was you and the other person. Everyone else in the building was witnesses.

Again, I am mindful of the error (maybe not) of my own way and I know looking back that I did not consider what was said as something that I thought that I would have to withdraw, but it happened. Now I want to make sure that it does not happen to others.

Anyway, marriage is a covenant and when we enter it we should see it for what it is. In fact, we should go over each one of the vows that we are going to speak to our partner and make sure that we are willing to live up to them under all circumstances and then think of the worst thing that can happen and see if you are willing to still be in covenant. The hard part will be to remove your emotions and feelings of love so that you can take a realistic look at the truth.

When God ordained marriage, it was in His mind that the couple would want to be together for their life time. He was thinking commitment and unity. He was thinking two people who would often have difference but not to the point of smashing the dishes. He was thinking unselfishness as he though how each party would always seek to please the other and in that way the relationship would be a "win-win" for them both. He was thinking that two people would come together and meet each other with love and always seek to resolve their issues for the sake of the marriage.

The marriage of two people is designed by God so that we each can grow and understand what it means to be loyal, committed, compassionate, temperate, and even self disciplined.

CHAPTER 2

Roles and Functions

The idea of roles and functions is not a new concept to marriage. In fact, if we are to understand Ephesians 5 and Ephesians 6, they clearly outline some of the roles and functions of a husband, wife and children.

When you consider the fact that in the beginning God made them male and female and that He created them interdependent and not independent, it is clear that roles and functions were a part of the plan.

To take it a step further, after the fall, God yet again spelled out what can be considered roles and functions of a man and a woman.

If I made a list of the various things that are consider as "man' roles or "women" roles, I am sure that it would be met with some opposition. Some would argue that what is considered in scripture as the role of the woman is obsolete in this day and time. Some would say the same about the roles outlined in the scripture for a man. It does not take a rocket scientist to figure out that there is a real problem when it comes to down to marriage as our society has far too many divorces. Considering that fact, one would have to at least gives some thought to the question of whether or not one of the issues is that many couples in this century do not recognize roles and functions in a marriage and that is one of the issues that makes for a marriage destined to fail.

Once I was watching a movie and the creature on the movie had two heads. They called it a monster. In fact, the people of the town were frightened of the very appearance of it and quickly ran away at the sight of it. Why? It was abnormal, unusual and unpredictable. That is the way that a marriage looks when it has no defined roles for each entity.

I understand the dynamics of our society now where there are families that have only one parent or there are families where the child often has to step up and be an adult because one or both parents are on drugs, but that does not excuse the fact that without roles and functions people would run into each other and crash.

There are many roles and functions in a marriage and it is my opinion that a husband and a wife should take the time to discuss what each person will be responsible for before they are married.

Personally, I admit that I am old fashioned and I believe that the man is to be the provider. It is my belief that working outside of the home should be an option for the woman and that her primary role is managing the home, but even if she does work outside of the home, it does not forfeit her responsibilities in the home.

So, what does God say about the role of a husband? Is he there to take out the garbage, fix things, paint the house or chase creepy crawly things?

What about the wife? Is the wife there to cook, clean, washes and take care of the children?

I think that their duties may include that and then some, and while the bible does not list every single thing that the husband and the wife are supposed to do, it does give us some idea as to where to start.

I have to call your attention to scriptures like Ephesians 5. It is clear from this that the man is the head of his wife. To be head does not mean that she is made to be his doormat.

To be head means that he has to take the lead position of being responsible and accountable to God for all that happens in their home.

For example, when I was a child my father would come home from work and one of the first things that he would do is ask if my brothers and I had enough to eat during our supper time. His motive was that if we said no, he literally would not eat until he made sure that everyone else had. That may be a little extreme to some, but is shows how committed he was to making sure that his responsibility to provide was met. He was willing to make the sacrifices necessary to do what God required of him.

We can say that God has placed a husband in the home because He intended for things to be in order and He was smart enough to know that someone has to be in the leader's seat. That does not take away from the woman at all. It simply says that God has placed her husband there to provide the leadership. When God was issuing the assignment that He wanted man to fulfill, he told her husband and expected him to go back home and implement the plan and together they were to carry it out.

I know that there are women that will argue that some men are not doing their jobs and that is why women have a hard time with roles and functions. I would have to agree because that is the case in many instances. On the other hand, it is still the plan of God for things to be done a certain way.

Husbands are to take the leadership role but they are also to love their wives. Read the scripture and you will see the primary responsibility of love is placed on the man. God goes so far as to tell a husband how to love his wife. It is so deep that doing it requires men to abandon themselves and truly embrace their wives with everything that they have.

One of the challenges of giving this kind of love is that some men have never seen it within their families. That fact does not make it any less of a requirement. A husband must make up his mind that he is going to love his wife unconditionally. That is difficult when you have not seen the model and it is difficult if you are living with someone who is often not acting in a manner that causes you to love them.

There is a reality that we as husbands must come to grips with and that is that at least two weeks in each month, a wife is going to be physiologically out of her norm. That is the week before her menstrual cycle and the week during her menstrual cycle.

During the time of a woman's menstrual cycle she experiences things like back pains, blotting, nausea, diarrhea, constipation, headaches, breast tenderness, irritability and mood changes.

With all these things going on in her body, it is difficult for her to be herself during this time. We as men have to understand her during that time and look pass those things that challenge us in an effort to not only love them at that time, but to comfort them.

The husband is also required to be the overseer of the home both naturally and spiritually. That means that he is not only to provide the things that are needed, but he is to be the leader in their spiritual growth. It is my belief that every husband should start the Morning Prayer and evening prayer for his family. He should select the time when he can teach them from the scriptures and maybe even call a simple fast for the family.

It is the husband who God is holding responsible for the overall success of the household.

Have you ever wondered why in the book of Genesis that God would meet with Adam daily and not the two of them? Could it be because it was the time when God would not only instruct Adam, but would give him his report card on how his household was doing?

The husband is required to also initiate conflict resolution. For a man, this is difficult because in order for him to do that he has to let go of his pride and his ego. That is tough, but it is the way that God designed it to be.

This book does not have enough space to list all the roles and functions of a husband, but I can sum it up by saying leadership and provider is what God had in mind when he gave him his assignment.

The women also have roles and responsibilities in the home.

The bible speaks of a mutual submission to each other, but he puts a little extra on the women in this area. The mutual submission is because they both are to treat each other with respect, but to the wife the level of respect has to do with honoring her husband enough to allow God to deal with him even if he makes a wrong decision.

I have been told by many wives that one of the hardest things for a wife to do is to know that her husband is about to mess up and not jump in and fix things. That is tough for a wife, but in the area of submission, the goal for her is to allow the husband to be the head and let God deal with him for his errors (unless it is something that is life threatening).

Truthfully submission is a response and not a role.

There are other roles that a wife has to do if she is going to be the help mate that God called her to. She has to nurture; she has to manage the household. She has to do many things that she and her husband must agree on, but the chief responsibility is that she respects her husband and honors him when he may not be honorable.

CHAPTER 3

WHAT GOD HAS JOINED TOGETHER

The statement found in Matthew 19:6 is one that is without question most misunderstood amongst believers and if not misunderstood certainly among the least adhered to.

Just what was meant by "what God has joined together let not man put asunder?"

To understand this statement we will first examine what Jesus was addressing during that time. As usually they were trying to question Jesus just to see if there was a loophole somewhere when it came to divorce. There were varying schools of thought. There was the Pharisaic teaching that used Deuteronomy 24 and insisted that a man could find anything that he did not like about his wife and divorce her. There was also the School of Shammai who interpreted the same scripture to mean a man could divorce his wife if she was unfaithful. There was also the School of Hillel that understood the passage to mean that a man could divorce his wife for any reason.

The interesting thing about Matthew 19 in which Jesus addresses this issue is that he took a different position and instead sought to reveal to us that the real issue here was not the right to divorce but that the highest order of God was that a marriage be joined by Him and that the couple be one flesh with just as much effort toward marital harmony.

It is not that God wants us to divorce after that we have married. Rather, as divorce goes, he allowed it because the hearts of the people were hardened and His grace covered them.

I am of the opinion that the will of God in marriage is harmony amongst the couple and to insure that he uses a term in the new testament called "equally yoked, '" which in my opinion is a prerequisite for all marriages.

Let me get back to the point of the statement, "what God has joined together let not man put asunder."

You would have to at least consider it a true statement if I said that this scripture implies that what God himself has put together, no man can put it asunder. The optimum words here I believe are "what God." That carries with it the thought that if a marriage is going to work as it should God himself has to put it together. That does not meant that there will not be time when the marriage won't be challenged. We will likely agree when you are putting two different worlds together there will be some challenges. What it means is that the challenges will likely be easily overcome and maybe even minimized because a divine component exists in the relationship.

Think with me for a moment and I want you to be honest. When you were seeking your partner, what were you looking for? If I asked you the question of what you wanted in a partner, I would guess that you would give me a lot of answers that may include beauty, money, stability, and so on. I know that a few of you would even list being born again as one of the qualities and

characteristics that you are looking for.

My point here is that most people seek a

partner that meets some human need and yet

human need is what always messes us up. I

am not saying that some of the natural

characteristic should not be there, I am

saying that it is the God ordained qualities

that will keep a relationship together but we

seldom start with those.

What if God gave you a partner that was physically undesirable by you but was everything that you needed as a help mate?

What if God gave you a partner that was less concerned about getting ahead in life (although he was a good provider) and more concerned about eternal life? What if God gave you a partner who may not be all that you thought women should be in the bedroom or even from a domestic stand point, but was everything that you needed in a help mate? Would you be able to recognize that God was putting it together and not you? Would you be able to accept the conditions of God if none of what your human appetite desired was a part of your mate? Those are questions that have to be answered by us all.

The blessing is that I believe that God does allow us to have a little input into who he joins us with (if He truly joins us). I believe that some of the physical things and even some of the financial things are options that God will listen to. I think though that the final decision of the "love connection" belongs to God because He knows what and who we need.

Needless to say, there are a lot of marriages that God never put together. I can make that statement because there are so many people that married without seeking God on who they should marry and if they did sometimes they did not wait on God to give them the "go ahead."

How do we know that God put us with someone? To be honest, I am not really sure.

I don't believe that there is any one way to gauge this. I think that the only indicator is that when two people can have in common their belief in God and when they can find a way to work through the challenges of marriage Gods way and both be in agreement. I also happen to think that another sign is when two people are together and they both sharpen each other. It is likely that they will not be alike in the natural but what each brings to the table helps the other person to grow without even trying to

change the person.

CHAPTER 4

COMMUNICATION

Here it is. This is one of the most important issues as it relates to marriage. I will be the first to admit that I had not made an "A" in this area in times past and even now I am seeking to become better at it, but if a marriage is going to work this is one area that has to be perfected.

I have found that Colossians 4:6 says, "Let your communication be always full of grace, seasoned with salt so that you may know how to answer everyone." This is a great saying and one that is worthy of remembering but it is not all there is to communication in a marriage.

When we talk about communication in a marriage we speak of an exchange of information or opinions. That is where the problem comes in. Most couples are either not communicating at all or they lack some of the vital skills necessary to do it effectively.

One way or the other, we must learn to communicate with our mate.

I often hear couples say "he does not listen to me" or "he does not talk to me." When we hear that we automatically know that there is a communication problem.

So how do we fix a communication problem? The first thing we must do is understand a few things about communication and be willing to accept them and practice them even if we are the kind of people who simply don't talk.

If you have been married any length of time it want be long before you realize that communication is important if you have aspirations of working together as a couple. When God created marriage, he not only had procreation in mind but he also was thinking that two could come together as one and do what one alone could not do. In His wisdom, he knew that in order to accomplish that the two would have to share ideas, disagree on some of those ideas and then intelligently discuss the differences and come up with a solution that fell within the guidelines of scripture.

When you consider the many problems that a couple will experience, I think it is fair to say that many of them come from poor communication. That is something that someone said, didn't say or something someone heard that really was not what was said.

The bible speaks clearly on communication and goes as far as to say that even though it is both the husband and wife's duty to communicate, it is primarily the man's responsibility to make sure that communication in the home is clear, effective and conducted in line with biblical principles.

Brian Schwentley in his article entitled, "Biblical Principles for Solving Problems in the Home," list several principals that I think are note worthy to those of us seeking to communicate effectively. They are as follows:

Honesty

If you really want communication to be effective, you must be honest. The challenge with being honest is that most people are so used to deception and lying that when the truth comes along, it is difficult for them to swallow and rather than appreciate it for what it is, often they are offended by what could actually help them.

For example, if your mate comes to you and ask you if an outfit looks good or not and in your opinion it is not a good looking outfit, what would you do? Would you lie and say that it is a nice dress or suit even when you know it is not? Will you tell the truth in love?

If you are the person who is asking the question and your mate says that it is not an attractive outfit, will you get upset or will you accept what is said in love and look at it as if your mate was trying to give you what was considered by them to be good advice?

The point here is that we must be both willing to accept what is the truth even if we don't feel like it is and then make a judgment call as to what to do about it.

There is never a good reason to not tell truth to our mates, but I understand that some people don't because of how the mate reacts to the truth. The best thing I can say to that is to still be honest enough to tell your mate that you would love to be honest and open with them, but you just want them to listen and consider what you are saying.

It is important to tell the truth in love. You will be surprised how much free your spirit will feel as a result of that and if you have a mate that is offended by your truth check to make sure that you are saying it in love and then pray and ask God for His intervention.

Openness

Openness is the ability to be free from restraints. What that means is that a couple must be willing to share anything with their mate. That requires two things. First it requires that each partner handles subjects and issues in such a way that the other person is not afraid to approach you on any matter. Second it requires that each person is willing to listen and to consider the other persons point of view even if it does not change the way he or she may feel in the end.

It is important that the family take the time daily to discuss whatever is on the mind of each person.

I have seen this at work in the homes of some of my peers. One of my friends in particular uses dinner time to discuss with the family what each person's day was like and what each person may be concerned about at the moment when they are talking. I noticed that the children were so opened that they shared information that was very personal and somewhat of an embarrassing nature because of the environment of openness.

During your time of openness it is important to clearly relay what you are trying to say to the other person.

I have notice in communicating with my fiancé, that sometimes what we say has a different meaning to the other person. It is during those times that communication is lost and usually the conversation is a little challenged. We both work hard on trying to say things in such a way that the meaning does not take on a huge difference in the mind of the other person.

It is also important that husbands and wives speak openly but gently and lovingly to each other. My fiancé will probably tell you that depending on what day it was, I sometimes got and "F" in that area, but I am growing and seeking God more and more on helping me do it 100% of the time. Communication should not be a puzzle it should be open and clear.

Biblical speech

This is another area that challenges us. There is a challenge for many couples to speak to their mate in a certain tone and manner as the bible suggests.

A husband and a wife are required to speak to their mate in a way that promotes healing and godliness. That does not mean that everything that comes from your mouth has a "thee" or a "thou" behind it, what it means is that we should speak to our spouses in a way that is loving and kind and that provokes a good response. Again, I have often missed it in that area, but I am getting better each day. Biblical words are words that seek to edify and build and not tear down. They seek to take the person to a new level and promote responses that are positive.

Anger

This is another area that I missed it in. The area of anger. I have to admit that there are times when my fuse is a little shorter than others but I am getting better each day.

On the other hand, anger is not a bad thing it is just often a distraction to clear communication. There are many scriptures that speak of the anger of Jesus and yet he did not sin. That is where the problem comes in. If I am angry with my partner (which is not necessarily an abnormal response) and I can communicate my displeasure without raising my voice or saying things that are hurting, then I am not in violation of the word of God. If on the other hand, I cannot do that then I am in violation of the word of God.

There are many reasons why people get angry but I don't think any of them are just cause to hurt our mates. I can encourage you in this area because I have messed up in this area in the past myself and I now daily seek to not make that same mistake.

It is unfortunate but sometimes our mate becomes the victim of our anger that actually was triggered by someone else. I advise you to seek God if you find yourself doing this and ask God to help you to heal and not hurt your mate. In fact, you can ask Him at this exact moment.

Those are just a few things that Mr. Schwentley has to say about communication.

I am also encouraged by a few tips that I found listed with the Equality in Marriage Institute and they are as follows:

1. Realize that no that no one wins" an argument. If you don't leave a discussion with a possible solution to the problem, then neither party has been successful.

2. Compromise is an essential tool to solving problems through

communication. Before bringing up a problem, make sure you have thought of ways that you can help solve it by mutual compromise.

3. Try to be positive when bringing up sensitive marital problems. Instead of jumping right into a discussion,

open by acknowledging
that every partnership
could be improved and
you'd like to take some
time and discuss the
things that are working
in your relationship and
the areas that could use
improvement. It helps
to start by talking about
positive things and then
moving into the deeper

discussion on problem
areas.

4. Be a "reflective"
    listener and make sure
    you understand what
    your partner has said.
    "What I hear you
    saying is..." is a great
    way to make sure the
    proper message has
    been received.

5. Feel free to use the "time out" card if the discussion gets too intense. If an argument gets heated and irrational, it is better to postpone the discussion to a time and place where effective communication can happen.

6. Make sure your body language, facial expressions and vocal tone are in line with your message. One study showed that 55% of the emotional meaning of what you say is expressed by your facial expression. While only 7% of the emotional meaning is

verbal.

7. Be honest, direct and focus on the real issue. If you enter a conversation insecure about making your point -- you probably won't make it.

8. If you can't come up with a definitive solution, at least try to

end the conversation on

a positive note like "I

think it's good we've

both shared our

feelings and we'll

continue to talk about it

and try to come up with

a better solution."

9. Don't ever be rude or

talk down to your

partner in a discussion

about your relationship.

Don't dismiss an idea

or thought as absurd,

but instead listen to

your partner's point and

then react with the

reasons you disagree in

a respectful manner.

10. Stay on track. If you sit

down to talk about a

financial problem and

suddenly other

emotional issues are

coming up, realize that

you may need to focus

on one area at a time in

order to create

solutions instead of

mere bickering.

11. Recognize when you

need outside help to

communicate

effectively. A

counselor or marriage

retreat may help solve

what seems to be an

impossible

communication

problem.

These are all great points to consider in

your efforts toward good communication.
There are so many ways to improve
communication in a marriage that I could
not put them all in this book. The main
thing is that you and you mate determine
the best way for you to talk things through
and make every effort to follow that
guideline.

I am confident that if you take the time to
talk to each other and not at each other, you
will see a difference in your relationship.
It is sad to say, but many infidelities occur

because one of the mates longed for someone to talk to and the other mate neglected to be that person so they turned to someone else for comfort not knowing that emotions and feelings can quickly get out of control when they are unguarded. Take time each week to talk and watch your mate see you in a different light.

CHAPTER 5

HOW TO FIGHT FAIR

If there were a such thing as a perfect
relationship it would be one where there is
never a fight about anything, but since we
know that no such animal exist, let's
assume that every relationship will have a
fight at some point.

I am not sure that a fight in and of itself is
too bad, but I do believe that a fight out of

control can be destructive.

If you are in a relationship, you will likely have a fight if you have not already. The key is to fight fair. Admittedly I have not always lived by this principle.

I was impressed with an article that I found written by Simon Presland, entitled "How to Fight Fair." In his writings he cites several ways to fight fair as follows:

1. **Face your fear of confrontation.**

   There are people who will avoid confrontation at any cost without realizing that escaping an issue does not make it go away. Confrontation is both necessary and good as it helps not only to shine the light on a matter, but it also frees the concerned person from the bondage of an unresolved issue. Although there are reasons that people avoid confrontation, I am of the impression that in a relationship confrontation is necessary but it is to be conducted in the spirit of love and it should have the motive of coming together for the purpose of a sound resolution to an issue.

2. **Discuss the Conflict As Soon As Possible.** There are couples who don't like to discuss their conflicts but simply sweep them under a rug. I will admit that often when we are upset, we tend to not want to talk to the person at that time for any number of reasons. I suggest that you and your mate discuss the

conflict as soon as is humanly
possible. The bible even teaches
that the "sun" should not go down
on our wrath. The importance of
discussing the issue right away is
that it will help you to avoid having
time to add other things to your
issue that have no place in the
present challenge. People often
have conflict and drag what
happened last year into it and that
has nothing to do with your present

conflict in most cases. Try to avoid that and discuss the conflict as soon as possible. How soon you discuss the issue is up to you and your mate. Determine a time frame together and stick to it and you will see the blessing and the benefit of so doing.

3. **State Exactly What Is Bothering You.** One of the most difficult things for couples to do is to state exactly what is bothering them.

There are times when you feel that you can't be straight forward with your mate, but that is not a good practice. The best thing to do is to be straight about what is bothering you. It is human nature for the other person to be offended or to try and defend their position at first, but after a few times it is likely that you mate will appreciate your stating the facts and will seek to work toward the common good of the relationship.

4. **If Y our Spouse Says You Do, You Probably Do.** I will let you in on a secret. Part of the reason that God gave us mates is so that we can sharpen each other for the glory of God and the common good of our relationship. That means that there are times when your mate will see things that you will not. It is during those times that they may point them out to you and just because

you don't see them does not mean that they don't exist. The best thing that you can do is to listen objectively and seek to make the changes that are being discussed.

5. **Avoid Personal Insults and Character Assassinations.** There is often the temptation to assassinate and insult when you are trouble over a situation. That is the wrong thing to do as it only makes things worst and sometimes causes your

mate to experience emotions that are not healthy in the relationship. Unfortunately I have done that in the past and now make every effort to do a better job in that area.

6. **Confront With Truth and Affirm With Love.** This means that a couple should confront the other person with facts and truth. During this process each person should state the facts and allow time for the other person to reflect and then

provide and answer to the issue. The next thing in this process is to affirm these things with love.

7. **Listen To Learn.** Listen to your mate so that you can learn something not so that you can attack them and validate your position on a matter. There are times when you are wrong and they are right and vice versa. The key is to seek to improve and in order to improve it is often necessary to listen to learn.

8. **Confront to Heal Not To Win.**

When you confront a person it is
necessary to seek to heal not to win.
I have also failed in this area as well
but once again, I am seeking to get
better. The key here is to seek to
heal the situation. This is not the
time to seek to win and prove the
other person wrong. Proving the
other person wrong does not do
anything for the relationship but
healing the issue does. It is often

said that no one cares how much

you know, they want to know how

much you care. Seek to show that

you care about the relationship by

seeking to heal and not destroy it.

CHAPTER 6

WHAT MOST MEN WANT & WHAT

MOST WOMEN WANT

This chapter is written so that you can get
an idea of what it is said to be some of the
things that men and women want in a
relationship. I can give you many scriptures
that will support my findings but got the
sake of time I will go right into the meat of

this chapter. Please don't hold it against me if I do not quote a scripture, but I think you will find that every word written herein is inspired by principles of the bible.

This chapter is not meant to be the only answers to the issues of what men and women want, but it is taken from my discussions with at least 50 men and approximately 60 women.

The truth of the matter is that what a man wants and what a man needs is two different things and what a women wants and what a women needs is also two different things.

On the other hand, since God gave us the ability to have free will and choice, He does allow for us to seek certain things in our mates that are beneficial and appealing to us.

When speaking to approximately 60 women who were willing to share with me what they wanted from a man, I discovered that there were many similarities in the answer to this question. The answers that I received are as follows:

1. **A woman wants security:** At the top of the list for women was the need for security. I believe that this is acceptable to God because after all He did make man her covering and it is my belief that every women has within her the need for security (often hidden, but it is there). A woman's need for security has to do with the need to know that she is safe not only financially but

physically and emotionally as well. Her greatest desire is to be in a position where she is worry free from the overwhelming cares of this life. Let's face it, she was designed an emotionally creature so it stands to reason that she needs to be assured that all is in place as it should be and that any threat to her or her children is minimized, if not eliminated by the man that God gave to her.

2. **She wants her husband to reaffirm to her that he loves her:** It is the desire of every women for her husband to say and not just imply with his gifts that he loves her. The affirmation that a man gives to his wife in the form of words go a long way with her. Gifts are nice but to talk to her and express to her how you feel is something that goes a long way with her. Not only does she need to

hear "I love you," but she also
needs to hear you say how beautiful
she is, how wonderful she cooks
and even how much she does to
help you fulfill your purpose.

3. **A woman wants understanding
   and forgiveness:** One of the hard
   things for men to do when things go
   wrong in a relationship is to try to
   understand. I have been guilty of
   this myself and God has helped me
   to realize the error of my ways.

There are times when women will do things that men don't understand and vice versa, but what a woman wants is for her husband to try to understand her. A husband who is seeking to understand his wife is not only following the scripture, but he is ministering to her in a way that no other man can. It is the responsibility of men to understand so many things about his wife. He must understand her past and how it influences her. He must understand the physiological challenges that she faces each month as she experiences her menstrual cycle and how it affects her hormones. He must understand how she affected by things different from what he is affected by and he must be able to adjust for the glory of God and for the sake of the relationship. I write this because as a man, I have had to learn these things from experience and even now, I get it wrong from time to time. To understand her means to evaluate the situation prayerfully and accept the things that occurs sometimes without judgment or passivity. Once a man had understood his wife, her next desire is that he forgives her. Forgiveness for men is also hard. It is hard because we have to work through our egos and then allow God to get to that side of us that

103

actually longs to forgive. It is there, we just have to get in touch with it. To forgive her does not mean that you will forget what happened, rather it means that you will allow yourself to overlook what happened and not hold it against her or even bring it back up in a negative manner.

4. **A woman wants to have communication:** Most men do not communicate in the manner that

women want them to. To most men answers to questions are often short or conducted with body movement like a shoulder hunch or a head nod. What a woman wants with regard to communication is really for the man to talk to her in a one on one discussion about the issue. She wants straight answers and not answers that are vague and can be taken to mean something other than what is said. She wants answers that are defined and not general statements and although this may not be the way we men often communicate, this is what she wants. A man who communicates with a woman on that level is a prize possession to her.

5. **A woman wants time for her and the children:** This means that a woman wants a man to spend time with her doing the things that are helpful when it relates to the

children. It does not take a rocket scientist to figure it out, but the majority of meetings, afterschool events and activities as well as homework are accompanied by mom most of the time. It is not that men are not interested in this; it is that we often don't think that we are needed in this capacity. A women wants a man to help with the homework, attend the PTA, go to the afterschool event if for no other reason, it shows that he is interested in the family affairs.

6. **A woman wants a man to listen to her:** Listening to women is more than saying "ok, I hear ya." What a woman wants and needs from her husband is undivided attention. This is the time when he takes the time to sit down with her and listen without interruption from the television, the children, his best friend or anything else. She wants him to take the time

to digest what she says, think about it and engage in a meaningful conversation about it. She wants him to focus on her with his eyes, ears and mind and then answer her in a way that she gets resolve to whatever the issue was.

7. **A women wants affection and kindness:** Why is it that when people see couples holding hands in public that they automatically

assume that it is a new relationship? I think it is perhaps some people have grown accustomed to the fact that as couples get used to each other the level of affection dies. A woman wants her husband to be affectionate. Affection means different things to different people. To some it may mean holding hands in public to others it may mean a simple kiss or walking up behind her or him and just simply holding them. It could mean simply lying in bed watching television together cuddled up in an electric blanket, but whatever it means to her, she wants it.

8. **A woman wants a man to share responsibility in the household:** This means that a man should share the household duties whenever possible. It is not a bad thing for a man to prepare dinner if his wife is running late. It is not a bad thing for

a man to help with the dishes if the woman is combing the children hair. There are many household duties that a woman would love to see her husband help her with. The key is to remember that you are now a team. I admit that I am old fashioned and I come from a family that outlined roles and functions in the household, but I am also a firm believer that it is not a bad thing to share some of the duties of the household whenever possible.

A woman wants a man who is unselfish: I
am reminded of a scene in a movie where a
young lady was told that if a man really
loved her, one of the ways to determine that
was if he would give you his last chicken
wing. Then next scene of the lady found
her in the arms of this man as they watched
a movie together, as it would turn out they
were eating Buffalo wings while watching
the movie. The scene shows that there was
one wing left and the man holds it up and

say, " you gonna eat this," and before she

could answer the question he had eaten the

wing. Does that mean that he does not love

her? I am almost sure that it does not, but it

can be mistaken as a selfish gesture. The

point here is that many women have

complained about their husbands being

selfish and vice versa. Women want men

who are willing to give of themselves and

who will share with them in a caring

manner. I know of many couples who don't

allow the other person to drive their car. I

know of couples who borrow money from each other and pay it back with interest. I know of couples who have items in the refrigerator marked "his" and "hers." As ridiculous as that sounds, it is real. When we are married we are one and the idea is to share everything with our mates. God is pleased when we share with others, but I believe He is pleased even more when we share with our mates.

9. Women want men who value them: I cannot tell you the number of times that I have heard women say to me that they don't feel valued by their husbands. Women take on different roles in the household and regardless of what role it is, she wants to feel valued. She wants to feel that whatever her contribution is to the household, whether big or small, it is valuable. Sometimes we as men don't always tell them how valuable they are and we assume that they automatically know, but a woman wants to hear it from time to time from us. Hearing that she is valuable has a lot of weight to it. Try it and you will see what a difference it will make in the relationship.

10. A woman wants a man of faith:

This means that a woman not only wants a man with faith, but a man who has a relationship with God. You may say that not all women want this in a man, but I will say whether they express it or not, all women have an admiration for a man who loves God. To a woman who is looking for this in a man, there is nothing like it. It presupposes that he knows how to treat her, pray for her, understand her and equally important, he knows how to lead her. When a woman has a man who loves God, respect for him is generally one of the things that come natural to her. She cannot respect God without respecting her

man from God. There is nothing

like a man of faith to most women.

Most of them want it, many of them

never get it, but when they do, it is a

thing of blessings to them.

We have discussed what many women

say that they want from men; now let's

discuss what many men say that they

want from women.

There are many things that men want

from women, the list below is simply a partial list that is drawn from my conversation with approximately 50 men.

1. **Sex, Sex and more sex:**
   Although this not necessarily the number one thing on a man's list, you can rest assured that it is at the top of the list of most men, particularly those who are sexually functional. Why? Is it because that is all we

men ever think about? Is it because we are just testosterones on two legs? No. The reality is that we men want sex from our wives because it is one of the things that tell us that our wives desire us. We have the need to feel that the woman is attracted to us physically and that is one of the things that does it for us. The other side of the coin is the fact that sex to us equates love. This is how we express love that we feel for our wives. It is not that we are out of control; it is that we have that need in our lives to be desired and to express love in this way.

2. **Men need affirmation from their wives:** Like women, men need their wives to affirm to them how great and wonderful they really are.

3. **Men need to feel like the**

provider: Once in the earlier stages of our relationship when I was just transitioning into full time ministry and my funds were low, my fiancé and I went to dinner. I knew in my heart that if I paid for dinner it would deplete my budget, but I really want to take her to a nice dinner so I was willing to make the sacrifice. When we finished our meal, my fiancé, knowing my situation and being the discerning women that she is, reached into her purse and gave me her credit card. I looked at her and I knew exactly what she was doing. She was trying to save my ego and at the same time show that she was willing to acknowledge that a simple thing like presenting the bill to the waitress would help me keep it in tact. Needless to say, I left feeling no form of

embarrassment or even a feeling

of being belittle because of her

efforts. A man wants to feel like

the provider, even if he cannot

do certain things for legitimate

reasons. The same thing does

not apply for a man who wants

you to pay for everything or

who wants to live off of you that

is totally different. Whatever it

may take to make your man feel

like he is the provider, do it and see what wonderful things it brings to the relationship.

4. **A man wants the image of his wife to draw him:** In most relationships, there is something about the person that actually drew you to them. It could be their hair. It could be their clothe or any number of things, but whatever it is you have to try to keep it up for him. I was

told by one man that his wife

used to keep her nails and her

hair done and that after the

marriage it seems she let it all

go. They were not having

money problems either; it was

that it seems she just didn't have

an interest in doing that any

more. He said it really changed

the way he saw her. He said to

me that when she was keeping

herself up the image he had of

her was that she was sexy and gorgeous and now he said she is just plain. How tragic this is but it happens. Men like to look at their wives in a way that brings that extra joy to them and usually it is the image of what they saw when they first met that keeps them attracted to her. Sure she will age and so will he, but does that mean that silk lingerie have to be traded in for

cotton gowns or for that matter
luring perfume for Ben gay?
The point is that every man has
an image of his wife that keeps
his attention. Keep that image
alive.

5. **A man wants to feel respected by his wife:** Respect goes a long way for a man. All men want to know that their wives value them and will adhere to what they are suggesting. I know that

there are times when women don't feel that men deserve respect and depending on the circumstances that may be true. The issue with men is that we want and need to know that our wives will go out of their way to make us feel that what we say is important and that as the household goes (all things being equal) we have the last say in the matter after discussion.

Respect means that the woman trusts the judgment of her husband and that she values his decision making ability as well as his plans and objectives for their relationship. Respect means that even if she disagrees she knows how to say it in the spirit of love and she knows how to get her point across with our being loud and vocal.

6. **A man needs to feel desired:**

Men love to feel that they still "have it." We like to know that our wives admire and desire us not only sexually but as a companion. We like to know that our wives find us charming and loving and sexy (I admit we have to do our part to draw that out). We like to know that we can still turn her head and cause her to smile. I admit that sometimes men stop doing the things that warrant that from a women and men we must be aware of that fact, but a woman who expresses her desire for a her husband goes a long way in our book.

7. **A man wants a woman who pays attention to him:** This means that a man wants a woman who will study him and find out what makes him tick. Many women could care less

about what makes a man tick.
Her interest may be that she
wants what she wants in the
relationship, but if you want to
keep your man, take the time to
learn him. Learn what he likes,
dislikes and what he will
tolerate. Learn what he responds
to and what he likely will
ignore. Learn what he is
interested in and what he is
about and take the time to show

him that you are aware of those things.

8. **A man wants affection:**

Believe it or not, there are some men who are in touch with their sensitive side and it does not take away from their manhood. There are men who like cards and flowers and nice notes from time to time. I have spoken to several men who said it was difficult for them to find women who would recognize that side of them that appreciated a love note from time to time or a nice card every now and again. Women, if this is your man, you might want to start putting those things on your to do list.

9. **Men want to be shown appreciation.** There are things that a man is supposed to do for his wife. Those things are often things that are a part of his

duties as a husband and a father, but it is the desire of most men to be shown that those things are appreciated. I read something somewhere where a woman and a man were arguing about an issue of concern to them both. The women said to the man, "I know you get tired of doing things around the house and paying all the bills." The man said to her, "I do them because I love you." Those words

changed the women forever,

because she realized that the

things he did were not a chore

for him but a labor of love.

There are many things that you

husband may do that can be

considered his responsibility but

does that mean you cannot

express appreciation? Take the

time to tell him how much you

appreciate what he has done.

It is difficult to include everything in this chapter that will describe what a man wants and what a woman wants. You would do well by discussing it with your mate and making the adjustments accordingly.

CHAPTER 7

THE FIVE LOVE LANGUAGES

One of the struggles in marriage is to understand each other when it is difficult to understand each other. Sometimes what you say is taken out of context. Sometime

what you do is taken the wrong way and

even not appreciated. The challenge that

God presents to us is to love each other and

to submit to each other as God requires in

Ephesians 5.

Author Gary Chapman in his bestselling

book, Five Love Languages provides us

with what has come to be known as the five

languages that people speak in terms of

their way of expressing and receiving love.

I will attempt to explain each language so

that you can both identify which one characterizes you and so that you can better understand your mate.

1. **The Language of Words of Affirmation:** To a person who is characterized by this language, compliments mean the world to them, but not just compliments alone but the one that you don't have to ask for. People who are of this origin driven by compliments and explanations of what the

compliment really means. It is important to this person that you not shatter them with negative criticism, but that you take every opportunity to provide them with the reasons that they are loved and appreciated. Doing nice things for them is ok, but what they really want is to hear you say it as often as possible. There is no such thing as too many times to them compliments are what they are driven by.

- **Quality Time:** This is the language that is characterized by a person who wants quality time. This person wants your undivided attention with our interruptions from anything that would make them feel second place. To this person, special moments and events mean a lot to them and any deviation from plans can really hurt their feelings. That is why there are times when you plan a date with someone and have to cancel it you find that they really made a big deal about the cancellation. You don't understand because things sometimes come up. To them it was a real issue. It is likely because they speak a love language that calls for quality time in their lives to take on special meaning.

- **Receiving Gifts:** This love language is not about the gift itself, but the thought and the thoughtfulness that is put into your effort. To a person who speaks this language what they are looking for is the fact that someone cares, recognizes their value and is in touch with what it takes to please them.

- **Acts of Service:** This love language is about the things that are often considered small that one does for the person. A simple glass of water is often what will make this person feel on top of the world. Ladies try pouring your husband a drink at the dinner table and watch him light up if this is his language.

The people who speak this language
appreciate the small gestures from
others that mean so much to them.
The simple effort to relieve them of
duties or anything that makes their
lives comfortable and shows them
your concern really drives them.

- **Physical Touch:** The person that
  speaks this language is not about the
  sex only. The issue here is physical

touch. Things like hugs and pats on the back as well as holding hands, is what drives this person.

When you think about it you can be with a person and make every effort to satisfy them only to frustrate both you and them. Could it be that you are speaking the wrong language to them? Could it be that your sexual advances and gifts are not what is wanted, but simply quality time? It is worth your while to take a look at the languages

and see which on your mate speaks so that

you can both share in what is need for each

other. I strongly suggest going on the

internet and taking the test of the languages

and sharing with your mate what the

outcome is. It will make your marriage

better and your understanding of each other

will certainly improve.

CHAPTER 8

THE MARRIAGE BED AND YOUR
SEX LIFE

The basis for this chapter is found in 1

Corinthians 7:3-5 and Hebrews 13:4.

It is in these passages that we are told that

we are not to deny our spouse when it

comes to sex and that we are not under

restrictions (all things being equal) when it

comes to the bedroom in our marriage.

This chapter is dedicated to trying to

understand the dynamics of sex and

marriage and it is my prayer that it will

help someone get a God perspective of how

things are and what a blessing the bedroom

can be.

It is common knowledge that most men are

more sexually driven than women

(particularly after a certain age). It is not

that men are out of control as some have

suggested, but there is a good reason why

men and women have different sex drive levels. This book could never explain them all, but I do want to take a look at a few reasons.

One of the things that I must say is that just because you are a Christian does not mean your sex drive is less or greater. I mean it is not as though God turned off or on your sex drive at the new birth. In fact, the sex drive belongs to the natural and God said that the natural things are a part of who we are as well as the spiritual things.

When it comes to sex, most men really need it. There are exceptions to every rule, but assuming all things are equal a man has to have sex for physical, emotional, mental and sexual reasons. Every man has two glands called the seminal vesicles and these glands produce the fluid which makes up semen. The semen is stored in the seminal vesicles until ejaculation is about to occur. The glands fill up and signal the body when it is time for them to be released. The body then signals the brain that it is time to release and the brain and the body both seek to release. This occurrence is said to be one reason why some men are grumpy at times prior to the release.

The second issue is the prostate. The prostate produces a fluid when a man is aroused that prepares for ejaculation. That is why there are times when men often feel the prostate getting tender and they say that they have "blue balls. (although sometimes this is an excuse to manipulate women for sex)."

Thus there is a biological reason for men wanting sex. The nature of a man is that he has a craving for sex that is often time out of control. On the other hand a woman seeks love. Her need and drive for sex are influenced in part by her level of estrogen, testosterone, blood circulation and other factors which may even include something known as oxytocin. Oxytocin is a hormone that is produced when a person is touched in a certain manner. It promotes a desire to touch and be touched. It is that hormone that causes us to feel good about the person that we touched or that touched us but it creates a bonding between two people. When a woman has a high level of oxytocin she is likely to be more receptive to sex. When this hormone is mixed with the estrogen in a women body, it creates a desire to be penetrated. Although these things are true, a women is likely not as sexual driven (generally speaking) as a man because her need is love. Women by nature seek to be admired.

The difference between men and women is that men seek quantity and women seek quality. To a man it may be valuable to him to engage in sex often. To women the value of sex is not often placed in the quantity but the quality itself. For women, love is the proof that she needs in order to be sure that her man is going to stick by her and provide her with the security that she needs. A woman sees sex as the proof that she is committed to the man (in most cases). For a man sex is that act that allows him to express his love, but it also says to him that she desires him, which for him is great for his ego.

It does not really matter what the women is driven by or what the man is driven by because either way, sex is very important in the marriage and the bible says that the bed is undefiled.

I know of couples who argue about sex (or lack thereof) over 80% of their time together. I cannot tell you how many times couples have come to my office and complained about the lack of sex in the relationship.

I watched sometimes as couples would try to justify their reasons for not being sexually active. Sometimes the man would say, "I work all the time, I am tired when I come home, "and the women would say, "he's not romantic, all he wants to do is jump up and down on me and five minutes later it's over." Although those reasons may be their realities, they can still wreck havoc on a relationship.

I will agree that sex is not the most Important part of a relationship, but believe me, it is definitely in the top 10 percent. There are so many reasons that I can think of as to why sex is important. The reasons may range from physical fulfillment to a way of expressing ones love and affection for the other. Whatever the case, it is important.

The other side though is that each couple will have a different level of importance as it relates to sex. It is best to discuss this with your mate so that you can be on one

accord with this.

CHAPTER 9

BLENDED FAMILIES

Proverbs 22:6 instructs parents to train up their children in the way that they shall go and in the end they will not depart, thusly placing the obligation of raising a child on the parents.

There are times when two people meet and one or both of them have children from a previous marriage and the task of raising the children from other relationships now becomes a part of the new relationship.

With this new relationship come the challenges of what is known as blended families.

What is a blended family? A blended family is a family where children existed prior to a new relationship and upon entering a new relationship two different families are brought together in an effort to live harmoniously.

Remember the show the Brady Bunch? This was a show about a man who had previous children, who met a woman with previous children and they tried to bring the family together as one. That is a prime example of a blended family.

It sounds like a simple task but it is often not.

There are so many things that affect or promote the success of this type family. Things like:

- How the children were raised before you came in the picture
- What the discipline involved in one family versus another.

- What the belief and value systems were before you came into the picture.

- How the children view you the newcomer.

- How much input your new mate is willing to give you as it relates to the children.

- How much influence the "ex" has on the child.

- What expectations have been expressed prior to marriage as it relates to the children and the home

and so many, many more concerns.

Either way though, when you marry a

person with children, you take on the task

of raising those children as your own and

any thought to the contrary is a step toward

a challenged marriage.

I know that usually in the beginning most

people fail to consider this because love has

them blinded to the reality of what is about

to happen as it relates to taking on the

responsibility to bring two families

together, It can be a beautiful thing when it all comes together, but please understand that it will not come together immediately in all cases and it will take patience, effort and time on everyone's part.

What could possibly go wrong you may ask? Well let's just say that the list is so long that I could not possibly write it all in this book. I can tell you though that there are a few things that likely will have to be addressed.

One of the greatest lessons to learn is that a

step parents love is a great asset and it

provides the child with encouragement and

joy, but it can never take t he place of the

love or attachment of a natural parent (

there may be an exception-but rarely). I

was in a relationship once and I encourage

the children to get the outside parent a gift

for both Christmas and birthdays. The

children were delighted to do that as it

seemed to give them something to make the

other parent aware of the fact that they

cared. I did this with no concern about

whether or not the children would do the

same for me as it was my thought that I

have to at all cost, make sure the children

continue to love this parent. At the same

time, I was fully aware that there was no

way I could or should even try to take the

place of the other parent. One of the

mistakes people often make is to try to

compete with the other parent. It is no

reason for this and it usually never works

out in the end.

When you are in a blended family, there is

a need to adjust to some of your losses and new beginnings. Things are not going to be exactly the same as they were and you are going to have to adapt to new things in this new relationship and so will the children. It is crucial that the new family is filled with love so that each person can identify the needs of the other persons involved, including the children. It will take love to overcome some of the natural tendencies to be insecure in the family. That means those feelings that a husband or a wife has that makes them feel that they are on the sideline because too much attention is being given to the spouses children (that does happen). There has to be a balance and until both spouses understand that it will likely take a special effort to accept, pray and love them until it happens (that's hard, I know but you can do it).

It is important that when you are in a blended family that each person takes time to write down their needs and at some point the family should come together and discuss them.

If you think that blending will happen overnight, let me quickly ask you to correct that thought. Blending two families together may take a life time or it may take a year, but however long it takes you have to be committed to seeing it through. One of the things that most blended families have to deal with is that they have to deal with the other spouse's divorced husband or wife one way or the other. If it is not direct contact, it will be indirect through what the children say or how they act. How do you deal with that, especially if it is a negative thing and not a positive experience? There will need to be a lot of forgiveness, overlooking things and prayer to make this work.

Are you committed to the marriage? The moments that you experience this, will determine that for you. Children benefit best when harmony is available regardless of the circumstances. Again, I no one ever said it would be easy, but it is possible.

Now, let's get down to some basic truths
that you need to understand.

There is no doubt that you will love your
new partner but that does not mean that you
automatically love the new children, nor
does it mean that they love you
automatically. That is the challenge with
new relationships, we want and expect the
new children to love us automatically and it
does not always happen. It takes time to
establish positive, trusting relationships .If

you really want the children to like you,

you will have to consider their needs as

much as you do your own and those of a

new spouse. I have two soon to be step

children and I can honestly say that we

have not had an issue with this because I

considered their needs as well as my own

and those of their mother. Believe it or not

children have needs and those needs must

be met in order to have a successful

blended family.

Children want to feel:

- **Safe and secure** – Children want to
be able to depend on their parents.
When a parent goes through a
divorce, often they don't realize that
the child goes through that divorce
too and they often feel let down.
When this happens a child is not too
eager to let a step-parent come into
their world without first feeling that
they can trust this person not to

make them live that feeling of being let down.

- **Loved** –They want to know that they are loved by the new person. You have to not only say you love them, but demonstrate it in your daily interactions with them and your spouse.

- **Valued** – I am a firm believer that a child has a certain place in a relationship, but at the same time I feel that it is important to from time to time get the input of the child in some of the decision making. I don't think that you have to ask the child about everything, but there are things that affect the child that should be considered as impacting to the child and therefore creates a need to hear the child's heart on the matter. This makes the child feel needed and a part of the new family. You have to remember that you are not the only one getting a new family, but the child is also.

Those are just a few things that child needs.
The point is to take the child in
consideration as well as a part of your new
family.

CHAPTER 10

THE MONEY ISSUE

There are so many places in the bible
that speaks of money as it relates to
your family that I cannot possibly list
them all in this chapter.

The main one that I would like to use is Proverbs 13:22. This passage says that a good man leaves an inheritance to his children's children. Although this verse implies a legacy to be left for those to come, it goes without saying that while you are in the process of doing that, your immediate family will benefit as well.

Having said that, I now turn to what have been one of the biggest issues in marriage and one that has caused many divorces. That is the subject of money.

When you think about it, in the initial onset of a relationship, love or infatuation clouds our perspective of what impact money really makes in a relationship. Say what you will but few couples have survived a relationship that was financially strapped. It is not a matter of being a gold digger in many cases, but simply that women have a

God given internal need for security and sometimes, men don't always understand that. On the other hand, men, who are survivors, are usually less apt to panic when it comes to financial challenges, but that is not to say that there is not a place in men that has a need for money as well.

Money is not evil. It is the root cause of many evils, but in and of itself, it is not evil. In fact it is necessary.

When it comes to money and marriage, there are really two problems that are the baseline of the issue. Those problems are:

- Not managing the money properly
- No having enough money to manage

Both of these issues are crucial.

When it comes to managing the money, one of the real issues is the value systems of the couple. For example, one person may favor

shopping for whatever they want, versus

shopping for what is actually needed. There

is a difference there. I mean let's look at it

for what it is worth from a practical

perspective. What if a man had nine pair of

shoes and all things were equal and the

family was not at a point where there is a

surplus in the family at the end of the

month. Suppose one day that he came home

and he had a new pair of crocodile shows

that he purchased because he wanted them

and the credit card had a little room on it, what would his wife think in most cases? She would have to be thinking that he did not manage the money properly. Why, because although there was room on the credit card or he may have had extra money left over, it was not practical as there was no real surplus in the accounts that would warrant that purchase over perhaps something that they could have benefited from more.

What if the wife did the same thing? He would likely have felt the same way. That said; it is important to understand your partners value systems and to discuss them so that you can both be on the same page when it comes to money.

There is also the challenge sometimes of not having enough money. This could be due to employment situations. One person could be out of work or it could be that there is simply not enough income coming in to support the lifestyle that you are leading.

I cannot tell you the number of couples that I have spoken to who live well beyond their means because one or the other feels the need to be in a certain status. It is better to sit down and discuss what is realistic as your budget goes and build your purchase around that than to live in a world where you are working just to pay for a life style.

One of the greatest lessons that I learned

was that it is better to live modestly and have money available than to live outside of your means and not have any funds available when you need it.

I am sure that some well meaning person may read this and say "God will supply all my needs." I totally agree that God will supply our needs, but by the same token you will find that the responsibility to be wise with our money (good stewards) has been given to us by God. If that statement does not appeal to you, it is ok because I am sure that if you live long enough and you see things any other way, you will find out that the statement is true.

The challenge for many couples is to take the time to consider the money issue as seriously as you consider every other aspect of the relationship.

In 2004, SmartMoney magazine did a study regarding financial situations with couples. The findings, in my opinion seem to suggest that there are a lot of considerations that need to be done when it comes to finances as couples go. To give you some ideas as to what could and should be considered when it comes down to the money in the marriage, I list the following:

- **Monitor your spending.** This is advice to both the husband and the wife. I will go as far as to say, take the time to discuss with your spouse what is appropriate to purchase without discussion and what is not. Consider setting a dollar amount as to what is acceptable and what is not acceptable without discussion.

- **Invest Wisely.** I used to think that when the going was great it was never going to stop until I woke up one day and it had actually stopped and there was no money in the bank. There I was basically penniless after having control over millions. How did that happen, I wondered? I quickly dismissed the question because at that point it did not matter how it happened, what mattered was the fact that it did and I needed to turn things around (God needed to turn them around for me). It was not a matter of bad investment in all cases, but in some cases the lack of investing into things that would likely continue to generate income forever and managing those things so that it would. My advice to you is to invest into something that will bring you residual income for the rest of your life.

- **Do not have money secrets.** I know it may be hard for you to believe that this happens between couples, but it does. There are couples who secretly spend money on things that the spouse has no idea about. That is not to say that each person cannot have a certain amount of money to spend as they like, but what if one person disagrees with the lottery and the other person secretly spends money on the lottery? We both know what is almost certain to happen when the other person finds out. The point is that when it comes to money, be honest with your spouse and seek to discuss things that will affect your financial picture. You will be surprise what a dollar here and a

dollar there spent will do to destroy
your goals sometimes.

- **Emergency Planning**. Whatever
  you do, make sure that you have an
  emergency fund available. If you
  can only set aside five dollars for
  that fund each month, please do it.
  The fact that you have a fund in
  place for times when it is needed is
  a weight off of your shoulders.
  Emergencies come up without us
  knowing when and where they will

occur from time to time. Having a fund available will make sure that when it does, you and your spouse want have that added to issues that are likely going to be topics of intense discussions during your marriage.

- **Discuss All Bank Accounts**. You would think that this goes without saying, but it does not. In a marriage you have to discuss if you want a joint account to handle bills and a separate account for personal use or whether you want to put it all in a joint account.

- **Deal with your debts.** Whatever you do take the time to discuss the debts that you have with your spouse. I have found that couples who don't discuss their debt before their marriage typically have issues when one or the other finds out about such debt. Discuss it and then decide what you can do to resolve it. More often than not, couples can come up with a plan to resolve the issue of debt together which makes for a better relationship.

Even though those things are good and practical way to help eliminate problems in marriage, you will find that from time to time you will likely face an intense discussion or two regarding this subject.

I was reading an article by Elizabeth Scott on About.com and she suggested that when these moments come, you can handle them by:

- Remaining Calm during times of intense discussion
- Get a clear view of the money situation of both people
- Focus on solutions to the problem
- Work together
- If necessary seek the help of a financial advisor.

Money does not have to be an issue in

marriage; it just is often because people don't take the time to deal with it. You can have a marriage that is free from the challenges of money by taking the time to carefully plan so that you cover all concerns.

I believe that it is the will of God for each household to prosper and to leave an inheritance and it starts with communication and planning for a successful outcome as your money goes.

I also believe that every couple should have a financial vision for their family. It is not important that you are starting out with little, what is important is that you have a vision to build something. People like John Rockefeller and Frank Woolworth started with nothing and now have empires. You and your family can do the same. The biggest trick of the enemy is to seek to divide you and your family and cause you to not have vision but "di-vision." When you allow that you strip away the potential for your family to eliminate money problems.

On the other hand, when you and your spouse come together and lay out a plan for your family's future that includes money, you are sure to make things much easier for all involved.

Money was designed to bless and not destroy you and it is up to us to have a healthy attitude about what God designed the money to do for our families. There is a plan for your family as money goes and it can start now if you have not taken the time to lay it our up to this point in your marriage.

The first thing to do (in my opinion) is to take the time to pray and repent for any erroneous thinking that you have done as it relates to your family and money. The next step is to have a serious conversation with your spouse about the money vision for your family and put your goals on paper.

Decide what part every person will play in the vision and make a covenant to do exactly what you say.

Take small steps until you can make bigger ones and understand that sacrifices have to be made in your process.

Most important of all, ask God to bless your plans and continue to pray together daily about your vision.

It will amaze you in the end as to what God

will do for two people who are unified and who really want to do what is right in His sight and the sight of each other..

Made in the USA
Columbia, SC
09 December 2024

47647638R00113